Christianity
in England

Linda Proud

And did those feet in ancient time
Walk upon England's mountains green?
And was the holy Lamb of God
On England's pleasant pastures seen?

WILLIAM BLAKE: MILTON

Above: *For the first Christians the attitude of prayer was raised and outstretched arms, as shown in this wall painting from the chapel of Lullingstone Roman villa in Kent.*

Jesus of Nazareth died in a Jerusalem ruled by the Roman empire. Within a decade of his death, that same empire had extended to its furthest reach, marked by a wall across northern Britain. With the Roman armies came the fledgling religion based on the life and teachings of Jesus. For the first few hundred years of its life, Christianity in Britain shared its history with the continental Church, suffering persecution under the Roman emperors until, in 313, it received official acceptance. There is literary evidence of an organized Church in Britain, with church buildings, but nothing physical remains that is earlier than the 4th century. It seems, however, that Christianity was a popular religion and grew up in Roman towns such as Dorchester, Silchester and Winchester. It was also popular with the landowning classes, and the villas of the Romano-Britons became centres of worship.

In such villas we find the symbols of Christianity fused with pagan imagery in a way that suggests the inhabitants experienced no conflict of faith, but absorbed one into the other. This suggests to some that British Christianity was not quite orthodox, perhaps as a result of the influence of the pre-Christian Druid faith of these islands.

St Alban, the First Martyr

The emperor Septimus Severus campaigned in Britain AD 209–211, and to discourage the Christian faith prescribed the death penalty for anyone converting to the new religion. A Romano-British soldier called Alban, stationed at Verulamium, sheltered a Christian priest during this period and was converted by him. Discovered and put to death, Alban became the first Christian martyr of Britain.

Above: *The beheading of St Alban, from the life of the saint written by Matthew Paris (d. 1259), the chronicler of the abbey of St Albans.*

Such is the evidence of literature and archaeology. Legend, however, gives another story. The man who provided the tomb for Jesus after the crucifixion was St Joseph of Arimathea, a tin trader who visited these shores. Joseph founded the first church, St Mary's, at Glastonbury, in Somerset. Here he buried the chalice Jesus had used in the Last Supper, and in which Joseph had caught drops of Christ's blood at the crucifixion, the chalice that came to be known as the Holy Grail. Glastonbury is therefore the heart of the grail legend and thought to be the burial place of King Arthur. Already considered a sacred site by the 10th century, Glastonbury Abbey grew to be the wealthiest monastic foundation in England. Though the abbey was violently destroyed in the dissolution of 1539, the continuity and vigour of worship in Glastonbury make it England's own Jerusalem.

Below: *The Tassilo Chalice, made for a Bavarian duke by English craftsmen in the 8th century. The Holy Grail, the chalice used by Jesus in the Last Supper, is commemorated by every chalice used in Holy Communion or Mass throughout the Christian world.*

Far right: *The Romano-British Christians drew on pagan imagery, as shown in this beardless image of Christ from the floor mosaic of the villa at Hinton St Mary.*

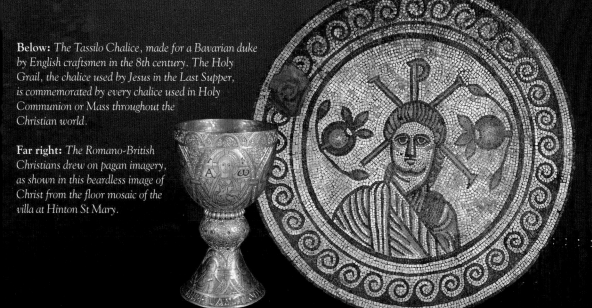

Deep peace of the running wave to you

FROM A CELTIC BLESSING

In the early 5th century the empire of Rome, internally weakened, fell to the barbarians. The invaders of Roman Britain were the Angles, Saxons and Jutes, who were to become the English. The papacy continued in Rome, however, and Britain came to the attention of Pope Gregory the Great when he saw some Anglian slaves on sale in the market. Impressed by them, the pope sent St Augustine (d. 604) to convert the English.

In response to the invasions, the British Church had retreated to those areas which had never fully come under Roman rule: Cornwall, Wales, Cumbria, Galloway and Strathclyde. With the founding of a monastery by St Ninian at Whithorn in the 4th century, influenced by the monastic tradition started in Gaul by St Martin of Tours, the Celtic church was renewed but it grew in isolation from the

Right: *Bewcastle Cross, carved by the Angles of Northumbria, has a runic inscription which reads 'of the powerful Lord', as well as panels depicting St John the Baptist and Christ in Majesty. It is a superb example of Northumbrian art.*

continent. Its abbots and saints lived the Christian life of simplicity, preaching by example. About a hundred years later, the Gospel was proclaimed in Ireland by St Patrick, a Celt of Galloway who was taken there in slavery. In the 6th century Christianity returned to Scotland with St Columba, who founded the island monastery of Iona. At the invitation of St Oswald (c.605–642), the king of Northumbria, St Aidan (d. 651) came from Iona to establish a monastery on Lindisfarne (Holy Island), from where he preached the Gospel to the heathen Anglo-Saxons.

Above: *The church of St Cedd at Bradwell in Essex dates from 652 and was made from the stones of the Roman fort of Orthona. Lacking skills in stone work, the Anglo-Saxons used Roman buildings as their quarries. Any inscription they found in Latin was used upside down to rob the words of their power.*

The Anglo-Saxons were Germanic warrior tribes who valued freedom, virtue and heroic acts of courage. They were also ruthless and ferocious. The teachings of Christ appealed to their better part and calmed the worst. With the courageous, evangelical work of the monks, the grounds of a common culture were seeded in these islands. How different was the Roman approach: organized, political, born of the Roman empire, St Augustine's church had been established in Canterbury. Through the efforts of men such as Paulinus and Wilfred, it spread from the south to the north. There were some obvious differences between the two churches, such as the shape of the tonsure (the shaved part of a monk's head) and the method for dating Easter, but the real difference was in outlook.

Above: *St Cuthbert built a cell on Hobthrush, off the Northumbrian coast, and retreated there from Lindisfarne.*

A synod was held at Whitby in 664 to try and resolve the differences, but the superiority of the Romans in argument spelt the end of the Celtic Church. Bede recorded these events one hundred years later in his *History of the English Church and People*. That his monastery of Jarrow had, like other monasteries, its cultural roots in Ireland, is evidenced by the wonderful illuminated Gospels, offspring of the famous *Book of Kells*. Such monastic communities were re-lighting the beacons of civilization in Europe, and Bede wrote as one in whom the two strands of Celtic inspiration and Roman discipline had merged.

Above: *Miniature of St Luke from the Gospels of St Augustine. This book, which came from Rome with the evangelizing saint in the 6th century, is housed in Cambridge but is taken to Canterbury Cathedral to act as an oath book at the enthronement of each new archbishop.*

Fire of the North

St Cuthbert, born in 635, was present at the Synod of Whitby to see his beloved church submit to the authority of Rome. After the Synod, ecclesiastical power transferred from Lindisfarne to York, but Cuthbert became prior of Lindisfarne and, eventually, a hermit on the Farne Islands, where he died. During the Viking raids of the 10th century, his relics were moved to Durham where the saint is still revered today, in the church he shares with his chronicler, the Venerable Bede.

*Free yourselves from worldly affairs so
that you may apply that wisdom which
God gave you wherever you can.*

ALFRED THE GREAT

Bede's era, called The Golden Age of
Northumbria, ended with the sacking of
Lindisfarne in 793. With that, and the subse-
quent one of 875, another dark age had fallen. This
time the barbarians were the Vikings of Scandinavia.
The last pagans of old Europe, they worshipped
ancient gods such as Odin and Thor; to them
island monasteries meant nothing more than easy
opportunities for pillage.

   Their raids began slowly enough for the learning
of Lindisfarne and other Northumbrian monasteries to be disseminated. A monk of York called
Alcuin (c.735–804) went to Gaul and inspired the
Carolingian Renaissance; St Boniface (680–754)
became 'the Apostle of Germany'. But for the
English – still divided into separate kingdoms –
such were the wars and deprivations that the lamp
of civilization flickered and almost went out. The
pressures of the Danes increased until, during the
reign of Alfred the Great (849–99) the fledgling
nation almost died.

   It was left to that
great king to save it
not only temporally
but spiritually, and,
in so doing, to lay
the foundation for a
nation. In making
many translations
himself of Christian
works, and in draw-
ing on the Ten
Commandments for
his laws, Alfred
revived both learn-
ing and religion. He
also made the first
tentative effort to
re-establish monastic

Above: *St Dunstan kneeling
at the feet of Christ, from a
10th-century manuscript.
The figure of the saint may be
a self-portrait.*

Above: *St Botolph's, Hardham, Sussex, is one of the last Saxon
churches built before the Normans and their culture swept
through Britain. The square east end is typically Saxon, and the
wall paintings are some of the earliest surviving in England.*

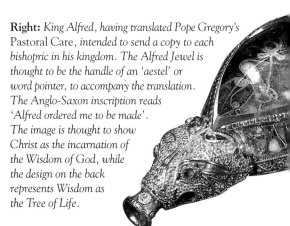

Right: *King Alfred, having translated Pope Gregory's
Pastoral Care, intended to send a copy to each
bishopric in his kingdom. The Alfred Jewel is
thought to be the handle of an 'aestel' or
word pointer, to accompany the translation.
The Anglo-Saxon inscription reads
'Alfred ordered me to be made'.
The image is thought to show
Christ as the incarnation of
the Wisdom of God, while
the design on the back
represents Wisdom as
the Tree of Life.*

communities, which had become almost extinct. As a part of his peace treaty with the Danes, he insisted on the baptism of his enemy Guthram. Thus, once again, the Christian faith was a means for healing a broken, divided nation.

Alfred's work came to fruition in St Dunstan (c.909–88), abbot of Glastonbury. St Dunstan reformed his monastery on the rule of St Benedict and Glastonbury became renowned for its learning. In 959 St Dunstan was made Archbishop of Canterbury and, together with King Edgar, he was responsible for a thorough reformation of Church and State. In Dunstan's 'renaissance' we see the light of Bede's world shining once again.

The last Anglo-Saxon king of England was Edward the Confessor (c.1003–66), the builder of the magnificent abbey at Westminster, who was made a saint for his piety.

From Viking to Christian King

Cnut (d.1035), the Dane who conquered England during the reign of Athelred the 'Unready', arrived as a rude and heathen chieftain. But consecration as the king of England affected him deeply, and he adopted the Christian faith as being the source of the civilization he so admired in England and the English. His famous attempt to turn back the waves was to demonstrate that it is God and not man who has power over nature.

Right: *Edward the Confessor depicted in the Bayeux tapestry. William of Normandy (1027–87) had his victory over England illustrated in needlework by the women of the vanquished Anglo-Saxons.*

> As I was walking round the cloisters
> I saw the brethren sitting together,
> arranged like a most lovely garland.
> And in the whole of that throng I could
> not find one whom I did not love, and by
> whom I was not loved.
>
> AILRED OF RIEVAULX, REFLECTIONS ON LOVE

The end of the Anglo-Saxon world came 60 years after the first millennium, when Duke William conquered England.

The Normans – or Norsemen – were of the same stock as the Vikings and were just as terrible in conquest. But by this time they were fully converted to Christianity, and Duke William brought continental abbots and bishops to transform the English Church. His own counsellor and friend was Lanfranc (c.1010–89), abbot of Bec in Normandy and a great teacher. As Archbishop of Canterbury, Lanfranc brought to English theology and scholarship the intellectual vigour of the European universities. His eventual successor was Anselm (1033–1109), also abbot of Bec and one who similarly combined learning with piety. Anselm was the originator of scholasticism and wrote with great clarity. In his clash with King William Rufus (c.1056–1100) he prefigured the struggles of St Thomas Becket.

If the conquerors gave new life and impetus to the English Church, the cost was the loss of the Anglo-Saxon saints, their names struck from the Church calendar, their bones pulled from the ground. That the remains of St Cuthbert survived the Norman onslaught, so that his grave may still be visited today in Durham Cathedral, was because the uncorrupted state of his body convinced the knights of his sainthood.

The simple goodness of St Wulfstan (c.1009–95) helped him retain his bishopric of Worcester after the Conquest. 'We labour to heap up stones,' he lamented, as his countrymen everywhere

Below: *The south door of Kilpeck church in Herefordshire. The travels of the Normans through Russia, Asia and Byzantium influenced the style of their architecture, particularly the rounded arch and zigzag or chevron designs.*

500 of them. They were particularly strong in the north of England, at places such as Rievaulx, Fountains and Kirkstall. Unavoidably part of the feudal society in which they were born, these monastic foundations grew immensely rich on tithes and on the acquisition of land. An abbey such as that at Abingdon was the size of a small town, while the diocese of Lincoln stretched from the Humber to the Thames.

Left: *St Edmund of Abingdon is shown here in stained glass from the Church of the Assumption of the Virgin Mary in Beckley, Oxfordshire. Born Edmund Rich c.1170, he became archbishop of Canterbury. Pious, gentle and mystical, he found himself in dispute with the temporal aims of King Henry III.*

Below: *Rievaulx Abbey from the air, showing the extensive land holdings that came with the great abbeys. The abbots of these huge monastic establishments suffered a confusion of roles not always conducive to spiritual life, though men such as Ailred of Rievaulx proved notable exceptions.*

Above: *Durham Cathedral, with its heavy, rounded arches and massive pillars, is one of the earliest Romanesque churches in Europe and marks the beginning of the great age of cathedral building.*

were employed in the massive building programme of the Normans. Using English stonemasons and builders, the barons stamped the land not only with their castles but with their cathedrals, parish churches and monasteries.

The flowering of monasticism in Europe was mainly inspired by the monks of Cluny in the 10th century and Cîteaux in the 11th, who had re-embraced the Rule of St Benedict, a humane, intelligent guide to the spiritual and administrative life of a monastery.

Cluniac abbeys and Cistercian foundations began to proliferate in England until, by 1150, there were almost

THE CHURCH MILITANT

Whosoever out of pure devotion and not for the sake of gaining honour or money, shall go to Jerusalem to liberate the Church of God, may count that journey in lieu of all penance.

POPE URBAN II

The history of England in the Middle Ages is entirely bound up with that of Europe. Wherever the Normans settled, they imposed a system of land distribution (fiefs) which they had taken from the Franks. Feudalism divided society into lords and vassals and introduced the notions of 'free' and 'unfree'. The Church became organized on the same principles, bishoprics and abbacies became the 'gift' of lords, and the men who held those offices were often more like barons than monks. But something in the function of bishop, archbishop or abbot, some hidden and pure authority, transformed some men, such as St Anselm (c.1033–1109), St Ailred (1109–67) and St Thomas Becket (1118–70), from lackeys of the king into men of holiness and integrity. Others, however, were only corrupted by their temporal powers.

Up until the 11th century there is no record of the Church acting with violence to those of other faiths. But with the call to arms made by Pope Urban II in 1095 all this changed. Jerusalem had been the ultimate destination of the Christian pilgrim but, since becoming occupied by Islam, it was hard to reach in safety. The first crusade liberated the Holy City but it proved difficult to defend. A second crusade, preached in 1146 by St Bernard of Clairvaux and led by the King of France and the Holy Roman Emperor, only made the situation worse. The loss of Jerusalem in 1187 inspired the third crusade but, despite the efforts of Richard I of England (1157–99), it was not regained.

The failure of the crusades caused men such as St Francis (1181–1226) and Raymond Lull (1235–1316) to preach the art of persuasion rather than persecution and thus mission was born. The Franciscan and Dominicans were organized specifically to travel abroad, carrying the Gospel.

Above: *Memorial brass of Sir John d'Abernon the Younger (d.1327), from Stoke d'Abernon. The duties of the land-owning barons included military service to God and king and many lost their lives in war.*

Below: *Alabaster effigy of Sir John Holcombe in Dorchester Abbey, Oxfordshire. He was knighted on the field of battle c.1270 but died of wounds received in the Holy Land during the crusades.*

The Terror of Inquisition

The idea of the inquisition still strikes terror, but its process was more drawn out than is generally thought and did not always end at the stake. A long examination gave the suspected heretic time for confession and absolution. Only if this failed was the accused interrogated and tried. The use of torture, at first rejected, was authorized in 1252 by Innocent IV. The convicted heretic would be subject to a range of penalties, from prayer through to life imprisonment. It was those who refused to recant their 'false' beliefs, or who lapsed again after confession, who were put to death, a duty that the Church left to the State.

Below: *The site of Becket's murder, in Canterbury Cathedral. The archbishop was killed by four knights, servants of Henry II.*

Above: *Salisbury Cathedral is a superb example of the architecture of the 12th century. The so-called 'transitional' style is marked by higher walls, wider spaces and rib vaulting. Rounded arches gave way to pointed ones, as seen here in Bishop Bridport's tomb.*

Left: *The Becket Casket, dating from about 1180, was made to house holy relics associated with St Thomas Becket. Though a fine example of Limoges enamelling, it was not this but its saintly associations that gave it celebrity status when it came up for sale in 1996.*

The love of the Godhead binds the mind of a lover so that he is not concerned about trivial things but is wholly intent on his Beloved.

RICHARD ROLLE, THE FIRE OF LOVE

At a time of popes and antipopes, and abuses of high office in the Church, many began to turn within themselves to find their faith. With the Black Death, the Hundred Years' War and frequent famines, death seemed ever present to the people of the 14th century. The threat of mortality was the very impetus of mysticism, which is the search within for that which does not die.

The vigorous strain of mysticism, still very much alive in English religion, can be traced back through St Augustine of Hippo to Plato and the Neoplatonists, who taught that the true reality is an ideal world beyond the perception of the senses. According to St Augustine the route of the mystic was a transformation of the person into Christ, and a full union with the godhead.

As mysticism lay outside the political organization of the Church, it was an area of the religious life in which women could be as active (or contemplative) as men. Of the great mystics of the Middle Ages, perhaps the greatest was a woman, Julian of Norwich (1342–c.1416). Thought to have been a widow, she spent the second half of her life as a recluse in Norwich. In 1373, she was healed of a serious illness, after experiencing a series of visions of Christ's suffering and of the Blessed Virgin. She wrote two accounts: a short version, written almost immediately, and a second, longer version, written 20 or 30 years later. Today her book, *Revelations of Divine Love*, a classic of English religious literature, remains an inspiration to Christians the world over.

Richard Rolle (c.1300–1349) attended the University of Oxford but found the scholarly method of studying theology inimical to the spirit. Leaving without a degree, he became a hermit and led a wandering life. It seems that he became a spiritual adviser to a community of nuns in Hampole, South Yorkshire; it was certainly for women, and perhaps for these particular ones, that he wrote his devotional prose in English, for often

Should any thought arise and obtrude itself between you and the darkness, asking what you are seeking, and what you are wanting, answer that it is God you want: 'Him I covet, him I seek, and nothing but him'.

THE CLOUD OF UNKNOWING

women were unable to read Latin. Today Rolle's fame rests on two pillars: his mystical experience, and his ability to express it so beautifully in his native language.

A contemporary of Rolle, Walter Hilton (c.1340–1396) left university to become a hermit and later an Augustinian monk. His *Ladder of Perfection* is a handbook for the contemplative life and shows how a soul may make itself perfect through contemplation of the image of Christ. Also of this period are *The Cloud of Unknowing* and *The Book of Privy Counselling*, two anonymous works written by the same author for those advanced in the path of contemplation. Their theme is that human reason cannot know God, but that the cloud which lies between Man and God may only be pierced by 'a sharp dart of love'.

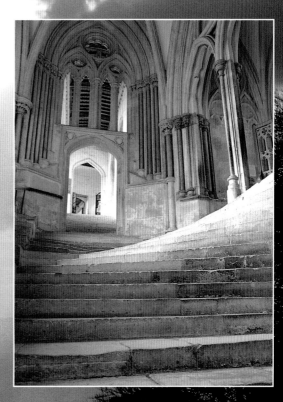

Above: *The Chapter House steps at Wells Cathedral, in Somerset, worn into waves of stone by the feet of generations of faithful pilgrims over 700 years.*

Pilgrims & Saints

Pilgrimage to holy sites, a tradition common to many faiths, reached its zenith in the 14th century, when people from all levels of society travelled to the shrine housing the relics of a favourite saint, in the hope of spiritual gain now and in the hereafter. Pilgrimage became a major element of medieval economics and churches with important relics grew fabulously rich.

Thank you Lord for my mind, and for those who can see into your mind. For my innermost self, and my ability to praise you. For my freedom, and the wisdom of the past which helps me choose well.

FROM A PRAYER OF LANCELOT ANDREWES

As Europe recovered from the devastation of the Black Death (1348–9), England found its own voice again. Up until this time, only those who spoke Latin or Norman French had been awarded high office in the State, but now English poetry was being written by men such as Chaucer and Langland, while at Agincourt Henry V roused his troops in English.

The scriptures were in Latin, a language unfamiliar to the mass of the population, and there came a need to have the Bible in English. But the Church was opposed to the idea, and the first

Below: *The tomb of Lancelot Andrewes, one of the translators of the Authorized Version of the Bible, in Southwark Cathedral.*

translators risked trial and punishment. The work of John Wycliffe (c.1330–1384) in translation was intended to make the word of God available to every man who could read, and was also part of his mission to reform the Church. His followers were a heretical group called the Lollards and the completion of his translation work coincided with the Peasants' Revolt of 1381. Wycliffe is considered by many to be the first Protestant but, although his works were condemned as heretical, he died a natural death.

It was over a hundred years before another translation was attempted, and in that time Europe had undergone the cultural transformation now called the Renaissance. With a flood of discoveries of manuscripts from the classical past, along with two generations of strenuous scholarship of Latin and Greek, a new air was blowing. Through such 'humanistic' studies came the idea that Man is in truth made in the image of God. In particular the translations of Plato, disseminated all over Europe, caused a radical review – and renewal – of Christian faith. It was no longer possible to accept dogma unquestioningly; with the use of reason, the devotional, sometimes superstitious medieval world came to an end.

John Colet (1466/7–1519), Dean of St Paul's, and his friend Erasmus (c.1469–1536) both travelled in Italy. Humanist scholarship inspired them to reform their Church, but they did not intend that schism which became the Reformation. Central to their thinking was the need to read the Bible itself and not commentaries on it.

William Tyndale (c.1494–1536) and Miles Coverdale (1488–1568) followed Wycliffe with a new translation of the Bible in lucid, graceful English. Although Caxton had established printing

Above: *Erasmus, a portrait by Hans Holbein (1527). In his desire for the laity to understand the liturgy and participate in worship, the Dutch scholar Erasmus set the foundations for the reformed Church of England.*

Above: *Fan vaulting in the nave of King's College Chapel, Cambridge, a fine example of the Perpendicular style.*

Below: *Tyndale's translation of the New Testament (right). The Great Bible, translated by Miles Coverdale (left). John Colet (centre), leading by example, advocated a Christian life based on a literal understanding of the Gospels.*

in England, Tyndale went abroad to publish his work, so as to evade arrest, but he was caught in Antwerp and executed in 1536. Within two years, however, Henry VIII commanded the clergy to install in a convenient place in every parish church 'one book of the whole Bible of the largest volume in English'. Known as The Great Bible, it was a combination of the work of Tyndale and Wycliffe.

The movement against the dogmas of the Church, which began to swell all over Europe, finally broke in the figure of Martin Luther (1483–1546). The Protestant Reformation had begun, and it was to be based on the word rather than the image. With the invention of printing, and translated into the vernacular, the word of the Lord became, perhaps for the first time, fully disseminated to all Christians.

'I am dying in the faith and for the faith of the Catholic Church, the king's good servant and God's first.'

THOMAS MORE

In 1534 Henry VIII (1491–1547) repudiated papal authority and established himself as the head of the Anglican Church. The cause was the pope's refusal to annul Henry's marriage to Catherine of Aragon, who had not borne him a male heir. Henry's second wife, Anne Boleyn, bore him a daughter (Elizabeth) and brought to England the French reformist movement called evangelism (from *evangelion*, Greek for 'gospel'), a name that reflected the desire to put the gospel into daily practice. Henry himself showed no desire to join the Protestant Reformation. It was Thomas Cranmer (1489–1556), the Archbishop of Canterbury and Henry's spiritual adviser, who

Left: The Book of Common Prayer, *the official service book of the Church of England. This edition is in the library of Winchester Cathedral.*

Above: *Martyr's Memorial, Oxford, by Gilbert Scott, commemorates the martyrdom of bishops Ridley and Latimer and Archbishop Cranmer.*

was to become the theological architect of the reformed Church in England. Ever faithful to the king, he wrote the prayers and litany that were to give the Anglican Church its distinctive voice.

At first the English Church continued with traditional forms of worship, and differed from Rome chiefly in the seat of its authority and in its liturgy, which was based on Cranmer's *Book of Common Prayer*. Its dogmatic position was defined in the Thirty-nine Articles of 1563. But as the Reformation and the Puritan movement gained ground, the old forms of English religion, which were vital, colourful and symbolic, began to

A Man for all Seasons

When Henry VIII made his stance against the pope, two of England's greatest intellects came to the defence not only of the Roman Church but also of Henry's wife Catherine. The king's Lord Chancellor, Sir Thomas More (1478–1535), whose judges included relations of Ann Boleyn, was imprisoned then beheaded for refusing to accept the king as the head of the Church. John Fisher (1469–1535) also refused to assent under oath to the Act of Succession. When the pope created Fisher a cardinal in 1535, the infuriated king had Fisher beheaded.

Above: *The ruins of Gisborough Priory in Cleveland. With the dissolution of the monasteries, Henry VIII swept away part of the medieval world. By the 16th century, the abbeys had become far removed from their original rules, but Henry's motives were more temporal than spiritual, and he seized their wealth to reward his supporters.*

Above: *The burning of Cranmer from Foxe's* Book of Martyrs, *a popular book of the time which vividly describes how Protestant martyrs suffered under Papist tyranny.*

disappear, its pictures and statues lost to whitewash or destroyed by Cromwell's iconoclasts.

The reformed Church flourished during the brief reign of Henry's heir Edward VI, but when Mary I (1516–58) came to the throne, she restored the Church of Rome and sent Reformers to the stake. Under the rule of Mary's sister Elizabeth I (1533–1603), however, the Anglican Church was revived and it was the Catholics who suffered. Meanwhile the people of England were forced by authority to a change that may not have been in their hearts.

By the Elizabethan Act of Supremacy and Act of Uniformity, the Church of England was established. However some English Christians, called 'recusants', chose to remain with the Church of Rome, despite loss of social rights. Although the translation of the Bible into English is strongly associated with the Protestant movement, in the 16th century the Roman Catholics also produced a bible in the vernacular, called the Douai-Reims after the French towns where it was translated.

Teach me, my God and King,
In all things thee to see,
And what I do in any thing,
To do it as for thee.

GEORGE HERBERT, THE ELIXIR

After the battles of Catholic and Protestant monarchs there was comparative peace during the reign of James I. In a Europe berated by reformist preachers, the Church of England used this period of freshness and quiet to recreate itself. A large aid to this, and perhaps surprising in the context of the time, was an advocacy of the use of reason.

It came from Richard Hooker (1554–1600), who wrote *Of the Laws of Ecclesiastical Polity*. Holding the middle ground it argued against both extremes: the Catholics, who found their authority in Scripture and Church tradition, and the Puritans, who found their authority only in Scripture. Hooker advocated a third way: that reason as well as scripture be a basis for action. Against the Puritans, who were loyal to the queen but not her Church, Hooker reestablished unity in Anglicanism by means of the trinity of Bible-Church-Reason, quoting Ecclesiastes that a 'threefold cord is not quickly broken'.

In the following generation, with people free to concentrate on their faith again, came a

Right: *Nicholas Ferrar commemorated in stained glass at the church of Bemerton, Wiltshire, where his friend George Herbert was priest. Here, in simple devotion to duty, Herbert spent the last years of his life.*

Above: *The chapel at Little Gidding. When Nicholas Ferrar bought the parish, the church was being used as a barn. The community restored it to its original use.*

revival of the mystical tradition. Nicholas Ferrar (1592–1637) gave up a career in parliament to create the first lay community in the English Church. Founded at Little Gidding, near Cambridge, it consisted of a group of about 30 people who lived the rule of prayer and work. The Little Gidding community was re-established in 1977.

A central ethic of the reformed Church, inspired by the Puritans, was that man and God require no intercessors: no saints, mothers, sons, images, churches – nothing but the Word, and the ear with which to hear it. Ferrar's great friend George Herbert (1593–1633) wrote poetry and hymns based on the patterns and rhythms of everyday speech. A contemporary and a friend of like mind was John Donne (1572–1631). Born a Catholic, Donne was to become an Anglican divine and

Above: *George Herbert at Bemerton, by William Dyce. The appeal of Herbert's verse, in its natural simplicity and sweetness, has not dimmed with time.*

Dean of St Paul's. Today he is famous for his poetry, but in his own time he was better known as a gifted preacher and writer of sermons.

In the light of humanist studies in ancient languages, a new translation of the Bible was begun in 1607. Herbert's tutor, Lancelot Andrewes, was one of several translators. This Bible, known as the Authorized Version, or King James Bible, was such a combination of scholarship and lyrical prose as to have a profound and lasting effect on the English people and their language.

Left: *The living of the church of Leighton Bromswold, five miles south of Little Gidding, came to George Herbert when he was canon of Lincoln Cathedral. Though he never lived there himself, but paid a curate to do his duties, the church captured his imagination in the richest period of his poetic life.*

THE PURITANS

Feed thy soul by meditation. Set thine hours, and keep them; and yield not to an easy distraction.

JOSEPH HALL, THE ART OF DIVINE MEDITATION

Left: *Oliver Cromwell, the son of a Calvinist, experienced conversion as one of God's elect. As a member of parliament he advocated the abolition of bishops and the ritual of the Book of Common Prayer. After the Civil War he sought to establish a Puritan republic.*

The Elizabethan Act of Settlement failed to satisfy the more extreme Protestants. Their desire for further purification of the Church gave them their name: the Puritans. They were not one group but many, united by a rejection of bishops and hierarchy, and it is from the Puritans that most if not all the various denominations and groups of English Christianity, which are neither Catholic nor Church of England, arose. A letter, *Admonition to the Parliament*, was the first manifesto of this religious movement which was destined to grow by the power of preaching and pamphleteering. The Anglican church, as designed by Elizabeth I, favoured moderate rather than extreme reform, but the Puritans wanted life and faith to be unified.

The Anglican church was and is the established church of England, governed by bishops with the monarch as its head. The conflicts of the Civil Wars of 1542–1651 were as much religious as political, with Cromwell's New Model Army largely comprising Puritans. To maintain its

Below: *A Quaker haberdasher and his family. As the Quakers put their beliefs to practical use in the field of commerce and industry, names such as Rowntree, Cadbury and Fry became synonymous with good employment practice.*

Above: *The poet John Milton (1608–74) worked on* Paradise Lost *and* Paradise Regained *in this little cottage in Chalfont St Giles, Buckinghamshire. Though nominally a Puritan, he showed much independent thinking.*

integrity, the Church of England needed strong characters holding its offices and, in the time of Charles I, the Archbishop of Canterbury was William Laud (1573–1645). Throughout the nation he strove to impose a form of service in strict accordance with the *Book of Common Prayer*. Some of the forms and vestments of Catholicism were reintroduced and he was dedicated to the repair and decoration of all churches in the land. To the Puritans, this all smacked of 'popery'.

Right: William Laud, by Anthony Van Dyck. Laud's inability to exact his reforms of the Church without arousing intense hatred in the Puritans took him to the block and left his reputation in ruins.

But Laud refused to compromise. Setting himself to raising the Church of England to a branch of the Church Catholic, he tried to separate puritan from orthodox clergy and to root out the former. His heavy-handedness in Scotland led to riots and, ultimately, to the death of the archbishop himself at the block in 1645, followed by Charles I in 1649. Under the protectorate of Oliver Cromwell (1599–1658), more radical groups emerged, such as the Diggers, the Levellers, the Shakers and the Quakers. Following Cromwell's death, however, the Puritans supported the restoration of the monarchy and even agreed to the Church having a (modified) episcopalian structure.

With the 'Glorious Revolution' of William III came the Act of Toleration of 1689. Though the Act granted freedom of worship to dissenting groups (although not including Catholics and Unitarians), it upheld those statutes which kept dissenters both politically and socially disadvantaged.

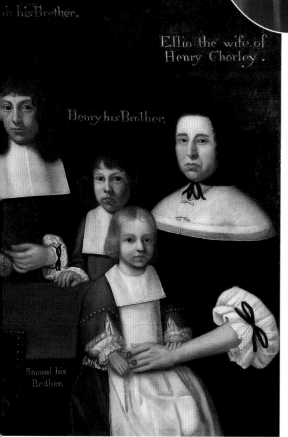

Above: *In the church of Patrishow, on the border of Wales, a medieval wall painting shows Death as a skeleton. Such imagery was a part of the instruction of a laity who could not understand the Latin liturgy. Following the translation of the Bible into English, however, and the rise in literacy, the text became the image, as seen on the facing wall.*

The Light is but one, which leads out of darkness and the dark world, into the world which is without end. Therefore, all Friends and Brethren in the eternal truth of God, walk in it up to God.

GEORGE FOX, LETTERS

What binds each Puritan congregation one with another is the emphasis on conversion by the Holy Spirit and the strength of each individual's personal relationship with God. Of the great number of nonconformist groups that arose in the 17th century, those remaining today include the Presbyterians, the Congregationalists, the Unitarians, and the largest of all Protestant communions, the Baptists, who promote baptism of adults rather than infants. The Quakers were founded by George Fox (1624–1691), who recorded that 'Justice Bennet of Derby first called us Quakers because we bid them tremble at the word of God'. The proper name for them is The Society of Friends. Fox, of humble background in Leicestershire, received

Above: *Interior of Wesley's Chapel, City Road, London, the 'Cathedral of World Methodism', where John Wesley (inset) lived for much of his life and where he eventually died.*

direct revelations of the Holy Spirit which caused him to become an itinerant preacher. The first Quaker congregations were established among the Puritan group called the Seekers.

Methodism, however, did not grow out of the Puritan movement but began as a Church of England club in the University of Oxford in the 18th century. The word Methodist, first used pejoratively, was coined from the methodical studies of the group led by John Wesley (1703–91) and his brother Charles (1707–1788). They held frequent communion, fasted, and were more eager in their religion than the average churchgoer. For this they were eventually cut off from the Church, but not until four years after John's death.

Above: *A Quaker's meeting in the 17th century.*

I design plain truth for plain people.

JOHN WESLEY: SERMONS ON SEVERAL OCCASIONS

Appealing particularly to the working people during the upheavals of the industrial revolution, the emphasis of Methodism became social work. The Methodist Missionary Society, founded in 1813, provided enthusiastic missionaries for work abroad, but Methodists were just as active at home in social and welfare reform. The Methodist Forward Movement, active from 1885, established several missions in the industrial centres of England.

Born of the Church of England, the Methodists may yet return to the mother Church. While discussions are being held about this possibility, closer links are already being forged in, for example, the sharing of church buildings.

The Wesleys were much influenced by the spiritual writer and mystic, William Law (1686–1761), author of such books as *Serious Call to a Devout and Human Life*. Stressing as he did the unity between God and Man, Law was more in the tradition of the early Church than the modern, and represents the continuity of mysticism into the modern world. In the same year its founder, Hugh Price Hughes, started the *Methodist Times*, the voice of Nonconformist opinions and social conscience.

Above: *A modern monument marking the site of Nettleton Court where John Wesley, attending a meeting in 1738, felt his heart 'strangely warmed' by the love of God.*

A Pilgrim's Journey

Born to an Anglican family, John Bunyan (1628–1688) became a Puritan during the Civil War. In himself he sought to expunge all sin and live the godly life. He joined the Bedford community of Baptists and became their chief preacher. During the years of Cromwell's protectorate, groups such as Baptists and Quakers had enjoyed freedom of worship. With the restoration of the monarchy, however, Bunyan was imprisoned on a charge of non-conformity with the Church of England. In prison he wrote the spiritual masterpiece, *The Pilgrim's Progress*.

WORKING FOR GOD

And did the Countenance Divine
Shine forth upon our clouded hills?
And was Jerusalem builded here
Among these dark Satanic Mills?

WILIAM BLAKE: MILTON

As the industrial revolution took hold, the needs of urban society began to proliferate. In England there was poverty, disease, child labour, a lack of employment, or too much employment in unhealthy factories; all the tribulations of people being forced from the land into towns by land enclosure and agricultural reforms.

Many philanthropic organizations, friendly societies and workers' clubs arose in response to these problems. The Clapham Sect, a group of Anglicans associated with John Venn, rector of Clapham, shared a belief that religion should be expressed in good works. Raising funds from the wealthy, they distributed them to worthy projects, such as that proposed by the writer Hannah More (1745–1833), who wished to start schools in the villages of Somerset in an age when education for working people was almost unheard of. Among her friends were John Newton (1725–1807), author of *How Sweet the Name of Jesus Sounds*, and William Wilberforce (1759–1833), the politician most associated with the Slavery Abolition Act, which was passed one month after his death.

Above: *William Wilberforce, by Sir Thomas Lawrence. Wilberforce, who was MP for Hull, was converted to evangelical Christianity during a tour of Europe. In his long fight to abolish the slave trade, he found support among the Quakers.*

A member of the Clapham group with Wilberforce was Charles Simeon (1759–1836). Inheriting from the Puritans a distaste for ritual, he led the Evangelical movement, or 'Low Church' as it was called. Simeon helped to found one of the major missionary groups, the CMS (Church Missionary Society) in 1799. It was the stated aim of such groups to carry the Gospel to the heathen, but much was also done in Africa, India and China in the areas of education, medicine and care of the sick.

The first missionary society was the SPCK (Society for Promoting Christian Knowledge), founded in 1698. Although English missions were most often associated with the Anglican Evangelicals, nonconformist sects also became involved. The Baptist preacher William Carey (1761–1834) wrote *Enquiry into the Obligations of Christians, to*

Left: *The writer Hannah More, by H. W. Pickersgill. More published many cheap pamphlets, advising the poor on how to improve their conditions through thrift and industry.*

Above: The Return of the Rev. John Williams at Tanna in the South Seas, the day before he was massacred. *Williams, sent to the Society islands by the London Missionary Society, initially met great success. Sixteen years later, however, he was killed by the cannibals of Erromango in the South Seas.*

Above: *Poster for an auction of slaves, 18 May 1829, four years before the Abolition Act. Three human beings are for sale, called Hannibal, William and Nancy, while several others are available on a letting arrangement.*

use *Means for the Conversion of Heathens* in 1792; at once it became the manifesto for Protestant mission, giving rise to the Baptist Missionary Society in 1793. Two years later, a letter that Carey sent from India inspired the formation of the London Missionary Society. The celebrated explorer David Livingstone (1813–73) was a member of the LMS, and had vowed to take Christianity into the very heart of Africa.

These were the days of inspiring heroes such as J. Hudson Taylor (1832–1905), who founded the China Inland Mission (1865); the Baptist preacher Charles Spurgeon (1834–92); and George Müller, a member of the Plymouth Brethren remembered for his work with orphans.

Right: *Lord Shaftesbury, by Boehm. A practical man of faith, the 7th Earl of Shaftesbury stopped the employment of women and children in coal mines.*

THE HIGH CHURCH

Let those who take pleasure in religious worship aim at inward sanctity.

JOHN HENRY NEWMAN

Above: *In this contemporary cartoon, Edward Pusey is shown as a moth attracted to a Roman candle.*

Between 1828 and 1832 a series of laws was passed in the British parliament of great importance to the Church of England in its relation to the State. Previously civil servants had been required to be communicants of the Church of England; at the same time, there had been many restrictions on Roman Catholics. These were swept away by the Catholic Emancipation Act of 1829, and many believed that there would be a rush of conversions from the Anglican High Church into Roman Catholicism.

The Oxford Movement, begun in response to these events, was founded by John Henry Newman (1801–90), John Keble (1792–1866)

Right: *Westminster Cathedral, a fine example of neo-Byzantine architecture, built 1895–1910, at a time when everyone, artists, poets and clergymen, desired the certainties of the past and returned to it for their inspiration.*

Above: *One of the most famous centres of Anglo-Catholicism, St Barnabas in Jericho, Oxford celebrates High Mass with a procession, incense and music.*

and Edward Pusey (1800–82). Inspired by the ideas of Archbishop Laud, they sought to give the Church an identity separate from the State. Also called the Tractarians, from the numerous tracts produced by the group, they soon came under attack from the establishment, the more so the closer the group drifted towards Rome. Eventually Newman was to convert and become a cardinal of the Roman Church.

The Oxford Movement, and its successor the Ritualists, promoted interest in the early writings of the Church and in sacramental worship. They encouraged the renewal of the monastic life for both men and women in the Church of England. With the High Church tradition, which arose from the Oxford Movement, came the return of sacred choral music, vestments and incense.

For many, however, and especially those who do not go to church, the image of the Church of England remains a medieval church somewhere in the shires, with dwindling but devoted attendance, Victorian hymns, flower arrangements dappled by light streaming through stained glass, and bells sounding out on a Sunday morning. For many churchgoers today, this is not reality.

Above: *During his visit in 1982, Pope John-Paul II attended Westminster Cathedral to meet the then head of the Roman Catholic Church in England, Cardinal Basil Hume. He also visited Canterbury Cathedral, encouraging hopes for closer ecumenical ties between the two Churches.*

Above: *Suffering transfigured into glory: Christ crucified, a sculpture by Helen Jennings in Coventry Cathedral.*

I will not cease from mental fight,
Nor shall my sword sleep in my hand,
Till we have built Jerusalem
In England's green and pleasant land.

WILLIAM BLAKE: MILTON

The Church of England today is a colourful range between the extremes of Anglo-Catholicism and Evangelicalism and all that lies in between. In our mobile and ever-changing society, people choose the Church that suits them best, rather than stay with the one they were born into or live closest to.

Numbers in the traditional wing of the Church have declined, particularly since the admission of women to the priesthood, a change that sent many clergy to the Roman, Greek and Russian Churches. The evangelical movement, however, reinvigorated by the charismatic movement of America, is enjoying massive growth. The centre of the movement is Holy Trinity, Brompton, in West London, which is also the seat of the Alpha Course, a ten-week introduction to Christianity.